Krampus the Beast of Christmas

& Other Similar Beings

Written by the Family Kim

Illustrated & Edited by N. Kim & using public domain/open source images

Front & Back cover images – own creation using public domain/open source images

First published in Australia 2024
This edition published 2024

Copyright© of the Family Kim 2024

The right of the Family Kim to be identified as the Author of the Work & has been asserted in accordance with the Copyright, Designs and Patents Act 1988.

All rights reserved. No part of this publication may be reproduced, stored in a retrieval system, or transmitted, in any form or by any means without the prior written permission of the publisher, nor be otherwise circulated in any form of binding or cover other than that in which it is published and without a similar condition being imposed on the subsequent purchaser.

The Family Kim
Krampus the Beast of Christmas & Other Similar Beings
ISBN: 978-1-7637546-1-4

About the Authors

For more information about the authors go to the website:

https://www.seeingbeingsisbelieving.com/about-us-1

Table of Contents:

1. Everything About Krampus - pg. 5

2. Stories About Krampus - pg. 9

3. Everything About Knecht Ruprecht - pg. 27

4. Information About Other Similar Creatures - pg. 32

5. Traditional Monstrous Recipes - pg. 35

Everything About Krampus

Before the beginnings of Christmas or Halloween, there was a festivity that combined the two, it was called Samhain, followed by the belief in Krampus or similar known creatures. The pagan people celebrated Samhain. Samhain was later changed to Halloween, sometime in the 18th century. Samhain was outlawed during those times, because of the Catholic church. The old Christmas folklore and Samhain as it is known today was not around that time frame, similar festivities may have taken place in secret.

Since the 1700s, every year in early December (Krampus & other similar creatures that existed a long time before the belief in St. Nicholas, he/they are also known as the first Christmas beings), children in Austria (and the whole alpine region of Germany & Switzerland) would get ready for St. Nicholas to visit them. If they've been good, he'll reward them with presents and treats. But if they've been bad, they'll get a lot more than a lump of coal–they'll have to face Krampus.

Who's Krampus, you ask? He's the half-man, half-goat who comes around every year to chase naughty children and maybe even drag them to hell. European versions of St. Nicholas have long had scary counterparts like Belsnickle and Knecht Ruprecht who dole out punishment. Krampus is one such character who comes from folklore in Austria's Alpine region (and the whole alpine region of

Germany & Switzerland), where he's been frightening children and amusing adults for hundreds of years.

Krampus and St. Nick's other bad boys (e.g. Knecht Ruprecht & many others) have their origins in pagan celebrations of the winter solstice. Later, some became part of Christian traditions in which St. Nicholas and Krampus visited children to reward/punish

them on the night of the 5th and 6th of December. In Alpine Austria and some parts of Germany, this day was known as *Krampusnacht*, or "Krampus night," when adults might dress up as Krampus to frighten children at their homes.

Children might have also seen Krampus running through the streets during a *Krampuslauf* – literally, a "Krampus run." If Krampusnacht was a way to scare kids into behaving themselves, the Krampuslauf, which isn't tied to a specific day, was a way for grown men to blow off steam while probably still scaring kids. Men would get drunk and run through the streets dressed as the fearsome creature. Like Krampusnacht, the Krampuslauf tradition continues to the present day.

The introduction of mass visual media couldn't help but sweep the charismatic Krampus up in its wave. When the postcard industry experienced a boom in Germany and Austria in the 1890s, it opened the way for *Krampuskarten*.

These holiday cards weren't mean to make you feel warm and fuzzy. Ones marked "Gruss vom Krampus" ("Greetings from Krampus") showed Krampus stuffing a distressed child into his satchel or preparing to hit one with his bundle of birch-sticks. Many of these postcards depicted Krampus going after children with his sticks, leading them away in chains, or carrying them off in his bag.

There were also cards that were a little more...adult. Krampus cards in the early 20th century show him punishing children, yes, but also proposing to women. In some cards, Krampus is portrayed as a large woman whipping tiny men with her birch sticks and carrying them off in her satchel. In another, a smiling woman dangles a defeated-looking Krampus in the air, holding his bundle of birch sticks behind her back. You can draw your own conclusions about the gender politics in these.

For over a century, people of the world probably never saw a Krampus card or even knew who Krampus was. That changed in 2004, when art director and graphic designer Monte Beauchamp published a book of Krampus cards and helped to organise an art show inspired by the cards.

Whether or not Beauchamp is primarily responsible for introducing Krampus cards to the new world, Krampus has since become a sort of ironic icon everywhere. Etsy has a whole section of items inspired by classic Krampus cards. And if you don't have time to send cards, you can buy an ugly Krampus sweater to wear to your local Krampus party or Krampuslauf. Krampus' popularity in the world arguably peaked with the 2015 feature film *Krampus*, which shouldn't be confused with the many other low-budget Krampus movies. Although Krampus is relatively new to the world, this alpine legend is the original bad Santa.

Stories About Krampus

A Krampus Story

Stefan opened his eyes, and he realised his body was cramped. He tried to move, but found that he was inside some sort of a rough canvas bag that scratched at his face and hands and feet. Sure that it was a bad dream, Stefan pinched his cheeks hard, but just yelped in pain.

He wasn't dreaming.

The last thing Stefan remembered was falling asleep in his bed. It had been Christmas Eve, and he was anxiously awaiting finally getting his first car. Even though he was a few years away from being able to legally drive, his sister had also gotten her first Porsche at 13, so he was sure he'd get one this year as well.

Thoughts of his new car vanished as he brought himself into the present. He had no idea how he had gotten into this rough sack, but he knew that he had been kidnapped. Stefan thought about his classmate Donald who had gotten kidnapped when he was vacationing in South America. He had thought it would be cool to be kidnapped, as you were only kidnapped if your parents were super wealthy or famous, but this was not cool at all.

Stefan tried to call for help, but there was no response. He struggled a bit, and as he pushed against the burlap sack, he could suddenly feel fresh air on his shoulder. Stefan curled up his body and tried to reposition himself so he could press against the small hole with his fist.

After managing to get his hand free, Stefan felt around and grasped a long piece of cord. He tugged at it, and after some time, the knot fell away and the bag opened up. The walls of the bag fell around Stefan's body, and he suddenly felt scared, as he was no longer obscured in his sack.

Even though Stefan was dressed in his Gucci tracksuit he wore as pyjamas & a skull ring he wore on his finger, he felt alone and naked, as he realised he was definitely not in a good place. The floor was made of cobblestones, and the only light came from a series of torches mounted on the wall. The stone walls were covered in black filth, and there were chains and shackles hanging from them. Mounds of dirty children's pyjamas and slippers littered the area, and across from where Stefan stood, it looked like a butcher shop out of a horror film.

Chunks of meat hung from hooks, and a collection of large knives hung on the wall above a sink. Stefan didn't realised that the handles of the knives were all repurposed bones, but he didn't need to in order to realise he needed to get out of there.

He slunk past a giant bubbling cauldron so large he would have to tiptoe to even have a chance of seeing into it, but he looked back at all of the kid-sized slippers littering the place, and didn't want to know what was being cooked. Stefan tried to step quietly as he moved through the cavernous space, sticking close to the walls. There were not many hiding places, but the shadows cast by the pillars along the walls were deep enough that he might hope to be overlooked by anyone coming his way.

As he came upon a doorway, Stefan froze. There was a narrow spiral staircase of stone steps leading upwards. Realising there would be no place to hide, and having no idea how long the staircase went, Stefan weighed his options. If he stayed, a bloody death at the hands of some unknown monster was certain. If he fled, he might get caught again, but at least there was a chance he might be able to escape before he was found.

Stefan took a deep breath to calm himself, and then began to ascend the stairs. The stone steps quickly became cool as he climbed, the heat of the kitchen fading quickly as he rounded the first bend. Stefan looked up, and all he could see were more stairs and darkness. There were no torches on the walls here. Stefan's heart felt like it was going to burst through his chest, but he knew he had to continue on.

Step by step, Stefan climbed the stone staircase, and his eyes began to adjust to the darkness the best they could. The stairs were so devoid of light, he could barely make out the next step, so he clung to the wall and moved carefully. He looked down, then up, and there was no telling how long the staircase went on, or how far he had come. Stefan sighed, but continued on.

Stefan had no idea how long he had been climbing the staircase. He hadn't counted each step, and with no way of knowing if he was close to the top or how far he had come, time had slipped away. His legs began to hurt, and his feet were almost numb, as the steps had grown icy cold quite a long time ago. Stefan had been sweating when he left the dungeon-like kitchen, but that sweat had cooled and dried, and now he found himself shivering.

Suddenly, he could see a faint glow coming from above, and a radiant warmth became apparent. Stefan's steps were painful, but he forced himself up quicker now, as the allure of the heat overrode his caution.

The higher he climbed, Stefan could feel the chill fade away, and he wasn't sure if he was hallucinating, but he could swear he smelled hot cocoa. Where was he?

Stefan followed the warmth and light and had to squint his eyes as the light became stronger. The young boy paused where he was, letting his eyes adjust to the light again after being so long in the dark. The stone steps were warm again, and he dropped down to crawl those last few steps. The staircase felt warm, and Stefan had half a mind to fall asleep there, cradled by its warmth after his long, frigid trek. Stefan slowly pulled his weary body up, step by step, and he peeked out from the mouth of the staircase. He saw a great hall filled with Christmas lights strung up along the high beams leading to the most massive Christmas tree Stefan had ever seen. It was covered in glistening blown glass ornaments and shimmering tinsel. The tree towered above all of the small, unattended child-sized workbenches and stools that sat in neat little rows. Along the walls were a plethora of giant fireplaces, all spaced apart so that the heat could be felt even from where Stefan stood.

Stefan looked around hesitantly, this new environment so different from the cold, brutal underground he had emerged from. The great hall was empty, and so he tentatively stepped out towards the nearest fireplace and took a seat.

The heat warmed his frigid body, and he slowly began to stop shaking. The feeling returned to his fingers and toes. The warmth felt so good, Stefan could barely keep his eyes open. Cradled by the heat, he wrapped his arms around his knees and felt his eyes begin to close.

'Hey there, friend,' a strange voice said.

Stefan's eyes shot open and he yelped as he spun around. Stefan saw a tall man with a kind face smiling at him.

'Sorry to scare you, I forgot something in the workshop so I came back to get it, but then I found you and I just thought you looked lost and could use some help,' the tall man stated.

The man was thin but muscular, and was wearing a forest-green vest and red pants. He looked young, but somehow seemed much, much older.

'Are you okay?' the tall man asked Stefan.
'Uh, where am I? Who are you?' Stefan asked unsure of where he now found himself.
'Well, you're at the North Pole at Santa's Workshop! My name is Rudolph, but you can just call me Rudi,' Rudi spoke plainly and extended his hand outward, Stefan tentatively shook it.

Rudi's hand was smooth as silk.

'Hi Rudi, I'm Stefan. Stefan Benson,' Stefan replied quietly.

Rudi smiled then said, 'Hello Stefan Benson. You seem quite a far way from home. I know not of any human families living nearby.'

A confused look came over Stefan's face.

'Ah, I am an elf, Stefan. As are almost all of the resident craftspeople here at Santa's Workshop,' Rudi said in a jolly voice.
'But, you look human. And elves and Santa don't exist,' Stefan stated sceptically.

'Ah, Stefan, you see, I most certainly am an elf, and I'm here in flesh and blood right before you,' Rudi said and brushed back his long silver hair to allow a giant, pointed ear to extend from its hiding place.

'Also, Santa is most definitely also real. I know it seems like he isn't, but it serves our purposes much more easily if most people don't believe it's so,' Rudi stated defiantly.

Stefan wasn't sure what to believe anymore. Was he really at the North Pole?

'Stefan, I'm sure all of this is a lot to take in, but let me show you something,' Rudi stated trying to reassure Stefan.

Rudi walked over to the stone wall next to the fireplace, and pressed his hands against the stone. The stone gave way as if it was made of liquid, and Rudi muttered something as he pulled his hands outward. The wall seemed to stretch as as newly formed window, complete with ornate grilles joining the multiple panes of glass, seemed to appear out of nowhere.

Stefan gasped as he slowly walked over. He slowly reached out and touched the icy glass. He tried make out some sort of buildings or signs of life, but all he could see was a world of swirling white snow and far off mountains of ice.

'Whoa, how did you do that?' Stefan asked as he stared at the window, then at Rudi, then back to the window.

Stefan pressed at the sill, the polished rock smooth under his hand.

'It's magic, Stefan. Craftsman magic, to be precise. It allows a skilled user to create new things out of old, like a new window where none was before. Or it allows us to make

toys for the good little children around the world,' Rudi tried to explain, then smiled beaming with pride.
'Wow,' Stefan said, smirked and stepped back.
'What else can you make? Can you make me a drone? Or a laptop?' Stefan said in a selfish tone.
Rudi chuckled: 'Slow down, my little friend. Before we get carried away here, we really should be getting you back home. Your parents are going to miss you.'
'Can your magic do that, Rudi? Can you make me a door that'll transport me back home to Illinois? Or can you make a teleporter gun that'll make a portal that'll get me back home?' Stefan asked out of curiosity.
'I'm a crafts person, Stefan, not some wizard,' Rudi explained.

Stefan frowned at this remark.

'My magic isn't nearly strong enough. I'm only 800 years old. In order to even attempt transcontinental teleportation, I'd need to be a few centuries old. But there is someone who can easily fold space and time, and that's Santa himself,' Rudi stated calmly.
Stefan smiled: 'So there's a way to get back home?'
Rudi shouted gleefully, 'Definitely! I'm not even sure how you got here, but whatever happened, I'm sure Santa will be able to take you back to where you belong!'
Rudi beamed a huge smile and then spoke, 'Why don't we head over to Santa's room and meet him now?'

The horrors of being woken up in the sack and the piles of children's clothes suddenly came back to Stefan.

'Wait, I was kidnapped! I woke up in some sack downstairs!' Stefan stepped backwards, suddenly suspicious of his new friend.

'Ah, Stefan, I understand. The caverns below this workshop belong to Krampus - think of him as Santa's counterpart who deals with naughty children. He kidnaps children and brings them here to scare them, then leaves Santa to take them back to their homes,' Rudi explained trying to calm down his new friend.

'But, I saw a bunch of kids' pyjamas and slippers in a pile down there! I've read the stories - he's eating them!' Stefan shouted.

Rudi laughed: 'Oh, Stefan, don't be silly. Those are the discarded clothes that the children have left behind after they've gotten their new holiday outfits from Santa. And yes, Krampus is also our chef who catches and butchers seals and fish and sometimes the occasional killer whale. As I remember, dinner should be served soon, and I think seal stew is on the menu. He doesn't ever eat children - his scary visage and mythology is just to frighten them into behaving better.'

Rudi smiled his warm smile again, and Stefan couldn't see any hint of lying. It did make a lot more sense. After all, if Krampus was really going to eat him, would he have really just left Stefan to escape?

Stefan smiled, and Rudi took Stefan's small hand in his own.

'Let's go meet Santa, shall we?' Rudi said and led the way through the joyous halls to a large red door, decorated with a beautifully lush wreath.

Rudi knocked at the door and spoke, 'Santa, may I request an audience? I have found a lost child, one of Krampus's abductees, I presume.'

The door creaked open.
Rudi walked in, but Stefan hesitated.

Rudi looked back at the cowering boy and said, 'Don't worry, Stefan, Santa will make things right! He'll take you home, come on!'

Stefan slowly released his grip on the door and walked into the room. The room was sparse, surprisingly so given the level of decoration in the grant hall. There were giant fur rugs on the ground, and a single fireplace that housed some glowing embers. Large candelabras floated in the air, suspended by some magical force, and in the far corner was a giant chair that looked almost like a throne. Stefan's eyes grew wide as he saw a giant, jolly-faced man dressed in a red robe with white furry trim seated there.
Rudi gently ushered Stefan forward.

The boy looked up at the massive man in front of him and said, 'Santa?'
'Ho, ho, ho, why hello, Stefan Benson. Welcome to the North Pole!' Santa shouted very loudly and let out a belly laugh, then smiled, his white teeth shining in the candlelight. 'I see our old boy Krampus has been up to no good,' Santa went on to say.

Santa stood, and walked over to the pair. Rudi was tall, at least six feet tall by Stefan's guess, but Santa towered over even Rudi. Santa was a giant, and Stefan understood why the door was so large.

'I found him in the workshop, sir, and thought you'd be able to bring him back to his home in Illinois, back in the United States,' Rudi replied to Santa.

'Ahh, thank you, Rudi, you did a great job. Also, good work on those stone fountains you created yesterday. Top notch masonry, and the electronics were well-done as well!' Santa praised Rudi.

'Thank you, sir, your praises are too kind,' Rudi beamed and bowed his head.

'Oh, Rudi, while I prepare little Stefan here for his trip back home, would you be a dear and gather up the rest of the elves? I believe it will be dinner time soon,' Santa said in a slightly menacing tone.

'My pleasure, Santa,' Rudi said naively, bowed deeply and turned to leave.

'Nice to meet you, Stefan. Have a safe trip back home!' Rudi said in a somewhat cheery tone to Stefan.

'Thank you, Rudi! Thank you for everything!' Stefan said in an unsure tone and waved to Rudi.

Rudi smiled, waved back, then turned and left.

Santa smiled, then waved his hand and the giant door slowly closed.

'Well, then, Stefan, let's get you back to where you belong, shall we?' Santa spoke, smiled, and waved his hand again, and a glowing blue portal appeared.

'Just head through that portal and you'll be back where you belong,' Santa explained to Stefan.

'Oh, uh, Rudi said something about new clothes as well?' Stefan stated quickly.

Santa looked at Stefan for a second, then smiled again and said, 'Ah yes, the new outfit. How could I have forgotten?'

Santa snapped his fingers, and a giant wrapped gift box appeared in front of Stefan.

'Why don't you try them on when you're on the other side?' Santa suggested to Stefan.

And with that, Santa pushed Stefan through the portal.

Stefan landed on a pile of warm laundry. But as he looked up at the ceiling, instead of his familiar blue ceiling, he saw moss-covered stone. He looked to his side, and realised he wasn't lying on a pile of laundry, but a pile of discarded pyjamas.
Stefan sat up, and sure enough, he was back in Krampus' kitchen. He realised that he was naked, his tracksuit crumpled next to him. The ceiling began to warp and twist, and Santa dropped down through the void. He walked next to the cauldron, picked up the giant ladle, and began stirring the pot.

Stefan asked in a scared tone, 'Santa?'

Santa stopped stirring the cauldron and walked over to where Stefan was cowering. Stefan noticed Santa had stopped smiling.

'That's my name when I'm up there,' Santa slyly spoke.
Santa's voice dropped a few registers as he spoke, his jovial tone turning into a bestial growl: 'But now, we're down here, right where you belong.'

Santa's jolly face began to drip off, and Stefan screamed. Stefan watched as as Santa's hair turned dark black and his eyes coal-red. Horns began to sprout, pushing back his red hood, as his lips seemed to fall off. Santa's teeth grew extended and sharp as a sickly, tongue fell from his mouth, lolling around like a worm.

Krampus stretched out his hand as one of the knives flew from its place above the sink into his hand. Stefan screamed again and didn't stop for a painfully long time.

—-

Rudi spoke, 'Santa?'

Santa looked up from his table to see Rudi staring up at him, Santa spoke, 'Yes, what is it, Rudi?'

'I was wondering - if you dislike Krampus' methods of scaring children so much - why do you let him continue to do that? Any one of us elves could easily take over the cooking duties given proper training,' Rudi asked Santa contemplatively.

Santa smiled his jolly grin and spoke once more, 'Rudi, as distasteful as it is, Krampus' methods do wonders to make sure children are behaving. After all, he only kidnaps children who are so twisted and evil that they're beyond redemption.'

'Beyond redemption? But Santa, don't you take all of those children back to their parents after their fear of Krampus has inspired a new way of living?' Rudi said in a confused voice.

'Of course, good Rudi, of course. What I meant to say was that if Krampus never got involved, these children would never be able to stay on the true, righteous path we try to inspire with our gifts. For the hundreds of children who might be encouraged to be kind and generous through positive encouragement, there are always a few who must be encouraged to curb their wicked ways through fear. It is not the way I wish the world to be, but how it is. Just think as Krampus as, well, someone who shares the same beliefs that I do, but just acts upon them in a different way,' Santa carefully explained.

'I see. But, what about Stefan? Was he really that bad?' Rudi asked Santa.

'To be honest, Stefan was not a good child. He bullied others and tormented many of his classmates. He had zero empathy for anyone but himself, and he was a manipulative, cruel little boy,' Santa replied in an annoyed tone.

'But, he seemed so nice,' Rudi said as his face contorted as he tried to reconcile the new information.

'Rudi, you haven't been out there to see the human world, but when they get in trouble, bullies are just like any other child. They cry, plead for help, rely on the kindness of strangers - but once they get an ounce of power, they start taking and taking and their greed and need for power consumes them,' Santa explained, trying to keep himself still. Santa walked over to Rudi, put his hand on the elf's shoulder and spoke, 'I know your mind is troubled, Rudi, but go have another bowl of the stew, and think not of Krampus and his unsavoury methods or the evils of the world. Go eat up, son, and let the meat give you the strength to continue on the righteous path. Just focus on all of the good children you're helping through your work,' Santa said reassuringly.

'Thank you, sir. I appreciate your time and guidance,' Rudi said in a happy voice and with that, Rudi turned, walked back and filled his bowl with another serving of stew.

Make your own ending or continue reading below:

Rudi went to get another bowl of stew from the cauldron. Once he had his serving in his bowl, he was about to eat when he spotted something floating in his stew. An odd, round shaped, slimy thing was in his food. Until Rudi realised it was an eyeball, that was just sloshing around in his bowl. Rudi was disgusted as well as scared at the same time. Now the stew was more ew than anything. Rudi put the bowl on the table, as soon as he placed it down on the surface of the table, he saw a finger floating in the stew, a finger that had a skull ring on it. Now it was obvious to Rudi that he had eaten bits & pieces of Stefan. The room was quiet, too quiet, even Rudi could notice this. However, he failed to notice a big, fat & plump shadow looming over him. Rudi turned and was greeted by something that looked like a combination of Krampus & Santa, with humongous, sharp & elongated white shiny teeth and monstrous looking eyes.

THE END

The Two Sisters & Krampus

Once, a long time ago, there were two sisters; one called Mary who was very, very good and one one called Emily who was very naughty.

And on one Christmas Eve, the Krampus; the goat headed monster that people say carries off naughty children, came down their chimney and stole away Emily in a sack, leaving behind a lump of coal to show that he had been there. But Mary loved her sister so much that when she saw that her sister was missing and when she noticed the lump of coal she started to cry.

When she saw the present that Santa Clause had left her under the tree she said, 'Whatever my present is, I do not want it. I would rather have my sister back.'

But then, to Mary's astonishment, she saw a label magically appear upon the present and when she read the label, it said, 'What is inside this present may help you save your sister.'

Mary, decided to tear open the present, inside she saw a golden pair of scissors, a candle of frankincense and a bottle of Myrrh. She picked up the scissors, the candle and the bottle and, immediately, she was transported to a dark coalmine, where she saw a chain gang of little children working with picks and shovels.

'Where is this place?' she asked one of the children, a little boy, who was digging with a pick.'
'This is the coalmine of Krampus where he makes naughty children dig coal,' said the child.
Mary told the little boy not to worry, that she had come to rescue all the children from Krampus and then she used the golden scissors to cut through the iron chains that bound the children as easily as if they were paper chains.

And, looking among the children, she found her sister Emily and hugged her, happy to be reunited reunited with her. Unfortunately, when Emily told her that the tunnels of Krampus's coal mine were like a labyrinth and only the beast knew the way out, Mary frowned.
Mary then for some reason lit the candle of Frankincense and, to all their amazement, the candle became a star, shining like the star of Bethlehem and, following the star along a maze of dark tunnels, Mary and the children found their way out of Krampus's coal mine. But then outside the entrance to the coalmine, they saw a room where Krampus was lying on a bed snoring, fast asleep.

'What are we to do now?' asked Emily.

Mary opened up the bottle of Myrrh.

'Myrrh is for anointing people with,' she said.
'So perhaps we are to anoint ourselves with it. And saying that she poured some on her hand and as soon as the fragrant oil touched her hand it became invisible.
'This must be to hide us from Krampus,' Mary said and proceeded to pour Myrrh over her head and the heads of Emily as well as the other children making them all invisible.

Then, being careful not to make any noise, the children tip toed across the room to the door of Krampus's house and, opening it went outside. Outside, they saw that they were on the top of a snowy mountain and there was no way down the mountain.

'We're trapped! How do we get home now?' said Emily.

Just then, however, they heard the sound of sleigh bells and then, across the sky, they saw Santa riding in his sleigh pulled by flying reindeers.

'Quick children,' said Santa Claus, landing upon the side of the mountain.
'Get on board my sleigh before Krampus catches you,' Santa said in a rushed tone.

And so Mary and the other children got onto the back of Santa's sleigh and then, tugging upon his reigns, Santa Claus made the sleigh rise up into the air and they flew off across sky.

'But Santa, why are you helping us? I thought that Krampus worked for you, to punish naughty children,' said Mary in a nervous voice.
'Don't believe everything you hear. Krampus is really my mortal enemy. Just as I was chosen by the powers of light to bring Christmas cheer to all the children of the world he was made by the powers of darkness to spoil Christmas,' said Santa Claus.

But then, suddenly, from behind them they heard the sound of howling and, turning round, Mary saw Krampus pursuing them in a sleigh drawn by a pack of flying arctic wolves. Then Krampus started to hurl lumps of coal at them.

'We're under attack,' said Emily as a coal lump went whizzing past them.

But then Mary picked up one of the parcels that were piled up in the back of Santa's sleigh.

'We can use these,' she said.

Then she and the other children started to throw the parcels at Krampus and Emily hit the old goat right between the horns so that he fell backwards off of his sleigh, plummeting to the ground far below. But then, as they were looking down, they saw Santa's workshop and, tugging upon the reigns, again, Santa Claus brought his flying sleigh in to land beside it. Then the doors of the workshop magically opened and they all followed Santa Claus inside. Mary and the other children saw all of Santa's little gnome helpers dancing and singing and having a Christmas party. The gnomes gave them all cake and ice cream to eat and lemonade to drink. Then they joined in the dancing and singing until they all started to feel very tired and Mary and Emily were sitting upon Santa's lap. They both started to close their eyes. But then, when they opened their eyes again, the two little girls realised that they were both at home in their beds.
'Did we dream it all, I wonder?' Mary asked her sister.

However, when Mary and Emily went downstairs, under the tree they saw two big presents wrapped in coloured paper and tied with ribbons, one addressed to each of them. Inside Emily's were lots of little dolls that looked like herself, Mary, Krampus, Santa Claus and all of the children they had rescued. On the other hand Mary's present was a picture book telling of their whole adventure.

THE END

Everything About Knecht Ruprecht

Knecht Ruprecht: Who was that again?

St. Nicholas fills boots with sweets and other gifts. But his companion, Knecht Ruprecht, is the evil counterpart. He threatens children who have been naughty with the rod. At least that's how it used to be. Knecht Ruprecht: Who was that again?

Since the 17th century, St. Nicholas has been known as the bringer of gifts. His figure goes back to two historical figures: the Bishop of Nicholas of Myra and Abbot Nicholas, who was born around 200 years later, who was from the Sion monastery, Switzerland. One figure who has been somewhat forgotten is St Nicholas' companion: Knecht Ruprecht. He has always been regarded as a terror for children, as he was the evil counterpart to St. Nicholas and threatened naughty children with the rod.

Knecht Ruprecht is treated as a creepy Krampus, especially in Austria and Switzerland.

Knecht Ruprecht? St Nicholas' Christmas time Companion

So much interest is given on Krampus this time of year, and it should come as a surprise for many to (except south Germany) to learn that many Germans aren't so familiar with Krampus. More common throughout Germany is the Knecht

Ruprecht figure. But who is Knecht Ruprecht? Is he a helper or a demon? And how does he fit into the St. Nicholas tradition? While the concept of Knecht Ruprecht, or Christmas-time 'Dark Helper' has been found for centuries, the name Knecht Ruprecht shows up on paper relatively recently. And he's one of the more familiar sidekicks of St. Nicholas.

Who is Knecht Ruprecht?

There are various origin stories for Knecht Ruprecht.
The word Knecht in German means servant or farmhand. And in a sense, he does act as St. Nicholas helper, since they travel together and he does all the sorts of heavy lifting. Some say that Knecht Ruprecht was a wounded foundling that St Nicholas rescued and raised. Others say he is a wild man (with horns) who comes out of the forest at Christmas-time, a dark elf, to help St. Nicholas. A more obscure legend comes from a story about St Nicholas. St. Nicholas arrived at an inn and discovered a horrible crime. The innkeeper had killed 3 boys and stuffed them into a pickling barrel. St. Nicholas brought the boys back to life and the innkeeper was punished by being forced to work alongside St. Nicholas as Knecht Ruprecht for all eternity.

Growing up, I was taught that the Christ kind brought gifts on Christmas eve and that St. Nicholas brought treats on the night of Dec.5. But like most German stories, there was an element of danger, or warning. A scary balance to the sweetness of and light of the benevolent gift-givers. And that was Knecht Ruprecht.

Who is Knecht Ruprecht? He's a wild man with a bushy beard, dressed in a hooded, brown cloak. In his hand he carries a large stick (all the better to beat you with) and at his waist is a child-sized bag....perfect for carrying off kids who have been bad! Some stories say that he has bells tied to his waist so that you can hear him coming (I'm convinced that part was added by parents who felt they still needed to instill fear, but who didn't have a costume....they could just get a family friend to ring bells outside).

When St Nicholas came to the door on the evening of Dec. 5. Knecht Ruprecht would be by his side.

He was the muscle of the operation, St Nicholas would open the big book to see if the devil had written anything bad about you. Then Knecht Ruprecht would make sure that you knew your prayers. If it was a bad year, he would give you a piece of birch tree rod or a lump of coal...or worse, stuff you in his sack and take you away. Kids who had been good, and who could recite the lords prayer (And maybe some other verses) would be given apples or nuts as a treat.

Some parents actually frightened their kids by having someone take them away to scare the heck out of them! I've read quite a few accounts of people who remember being taken or having a sibling been taken out to the woods for a good scare!
I cannot imagine flying with child protective services these days!!!

Although tales of St Nicholas helper had been around for ages, it wasn't until the 17th century, after the protestant reformation that he is mentioned on paper by name as Knecht Ruprecht in Nuremburg. There he is listed as part of the Christmas procession; the perfect balance for the sweet innocence of the Christ kind. (Christ kind can't possibly punish bad children!).

Dark and scary stories are not unusual in Germany. Using threats of dire consequences was the standard way to keep kids in line. Take a look at the original Grimm's fairy tales.
And remember that struwwelpeter was written because

Heinrich Hoffman couldn't find a book for his three year old that had the correct moral teachings. These dark stories come from a time when the world was a scary place. The woods were dark and dangerous, starvation was a reality.

Regional Variations

Knecht Ruprecht's appearance and activities vary considerably across different regions in Germany. In some areas, he is a solitary figure who visits homes alone, while in others, he accompanies St. Nicholas. His portrayal ranges from a horned, devil-like creature in some Alpine traditions to a more benign, fatherly figure in northern Germany.

Information About Other Similar Creatures

Krampus & Knecht Ruprecht Are Not Alone

If you think Krampus & Knecht Ruprecht are the only Christmas demon out there, you've probably been hiding in your gingerbread house for too long. Turns out, there's a world of terrifying holiday figures just waiting to beat you into obedience.

For instance, also in the land of Krampus (I guess he's pretty good at sharing) there's a witch named Frau Perchta who's known to, if you're a real piece of work, rip out your guts and replace them with garbage. Lovely.

Then there's Belsnickel of southwestern Germany who hands out both candy and whippings depending on your tendency towards misbehaving.

There's Hans Trapp, the French Satan worshipper who lives in the forest but comes out just before Christmas, dressed as a scarecrow, to scare children - (crows, oddly) into being good.

You've also got Jòlakötturinn, the Icelandic Christmas cat who may very well eat you if you don't do your chores, unless you behave good. On the other hand, he rewards the hard workers with new clothes, so that's nice.

Iceland also gives us Gryla, the ogress who kidnaps, cooks, and eats children who disobey their parents. To appease all these variations of beings, you can serve them according to folklore schnapps.

Traditional Monstrous Recipes

Krampus Bread

Every year on December 6th, people celebrate Saint Nicolas. The tradition goes like this. Kids place their boots in front of the home, and if they behave well, they get a small present; if they do not, they get a thin wooden stick in the boot. We always got a little gift and a small wooden stick. Krampus Bread, is a beautiful German& Slovenian/ European tradition. Every year you can bake little Krampuses for your kids. The bread is soft and delicious.

How long does it take?

Makes: 6 Krampus Bread (6 x 80g)

Preparation: 15 minutes

Proofing: 1 hour 30 minutes

Baking time : 20 minutes

Total time: 1hr 35 minutes

1. Ingredients: - Krampus Bread

- 450 g (1 pound) all-purpose flour

- 7 g (2 ¼ tsp) active dry yeast

- 50 g (1/4 cup) sugar

- 8 g (1 1/2 tsp) salt

- 250 ml (1 cup) milk

- 1 egg

- 60 g (1 stick) unsalted butter, cold

- Raisins, for the eyes and buttons

- Milk, for brushing

Tools and equipment:

- Bowl

- Stand mixer or hand-held mixer

- Large baking sheet

- Parchment paper

- Rolling pin

2. Method

Dough and proofing

Add all dry ingredients (all-purpose flour, yeast, sugar, and salt) to a large bowl or stand mixer bowl. Pour in the lukewarm milk and add an egg. Knead into a smooth dough using a stand mixer with a dough hook attachment or a hand-held mixer with two dough hooks–Knead for 5 minutes or until the dough is soft and elastic. Add the cold butter, cut it into cubes, and knead until the butter is incorporated. Cover the bowl with a kitchen towel or clingfilm and leave it to proof at room temperature for 45 minutes.

3. Shaping and second proofing

Divide the dough into four parts. Lightly dust your working surface and shape each piece of dough into a ball. Set aside for 10 minutes. Roll each ball into a 20 cm x 10 cm (8-inch x 4-inch) rectangle. Using a sharp knife, cut out the Krampus and lightly stretch it with your fingers–place it on a parchment-paper-lined large baking sheet. Using the leftover dough, shape it into two balls and repeat the shaping process. Make a small challah or bread roll if you have any additional leftovers. Cover the baking sheet with a kitchen towel or clingfilm. Leave the dough to proof at room temperature for 45 - 60 minutes or until visibly risen. Cut the large raisins in half. Add the raisins into a small bowl and cover them with 100ml (1/2 cup) of boiling water. Set aside until needed. Place a rack in the middle of the oven and preheat it to 190 °C / 375 °F.

4. Bake

When the Krampus bread is risen, evenly brush it with milk. Press the raisins into the dough to get two eyes and two buttons. Using scissors make a small incision to make the mouth. Place in the oven and bake for 17 - 20 minutes at 190 °C / 375 °F or until golden-brown.

Storing and freezing

You can store the Krampus Bread in two ways.

Keep it in a bread bag at room temperature for 2 days. The bread is softest the same day; however, it will be just as delicious the next day.

OR

Freeze the Krampus bread ahead. Store the baked and cooled bread in a freezer bag. Place in the freezer for up to a month.

Shaping

Shape the Krampus Bread in two ways.

You can use a sharp knife to shape Krampus bread or use a gingerbread man cookie cutter for easier cutting. You would still have to cut out the head, but at least the shaping will be easier.

Optionally, make the Krampus Bread without the egg. In that case, use 50 ml more liquid (water or milk).

Weckmänner

A simple and tasty recipe for a traditional German baked good. Eat it now, when they are customarily eaten or at any time that you just want some comfort.

St Martin

Weckmänner supposedly resemble St Martin and are eaten around St Martins Day (11 November). In some areas, they are said to resemble St Nicolaus and are eaten until 6 December. Both were bishops.

Weckmann literally means 'wake man', more traditionally 'watchman'. Weckmänner is the German plural of Weckmann. They are also known as Stutenkerle, Piepenkerle, Hefekerle, Kloskaehlsche, Printenmänner, Hanselmänner, Klasenmänner or Jahresmänner, depending on where you live in Germany. In essence the Weckmann bread is the same as the Krampus bread, however, the Weckmann bread became the christianised version opposite to the Krampus bread, because of Knecht Ruprecht.

The pipes

The clay pipe that the Weckmänner traditionally hold is supposed to resemble the bishop's crosier. How did the crosier become a pipe? No one is really sure.

Unless you live in Germany, you will probably find it difficult to get the 'pipe'. Even if you do live in Germany, the pipes are not that easy to obtain.

They will still taste the same without the pipe. It also leaves more space for buttons, if that is what you wish.

How long does it take?

Prep time: 50 minutes

Cook time: 20 minutes

Total time: 1hr 10 minutes

Cuisine: German

Serves: 9 people

Equipment:

- Mixing bowl

- Large gingerbread man cookie cutter

- Clay pipes

- Pastry brush

- Baking tray

- Baking paper

Ingredients:

- 1,500 g flour

- 3 packet or cube of yeast

- 750 ml lukewarm milk

- 375 g melted butter

- 300 g fine sugar

- Grated rind from half an orange

- 1.5 tsp. vanilla sugar or essence

- 3 egg size L or XL

- 3 egg yolk

- 3 good pinch of salt

- Raisins for eyes and buttons if desired

- Extra flour to flour the board

- Milk for brushing

Instructions

Activate the yeast: crumble the yeast into a bowl and add the milk and 1 tbsp. of the sugar and let it stand for a few minutes. The milk will start to go frothy and the yeast will start to spread.

Add the other ingredients and mix with your hand until all is combined.

Cover and put somewhere warm to proof until the dough has doubled in size.

Preheat the oven to 180°c fan-forced.

Turn out onto a floured board and use your fingers to flatten and spread until about 2-3 cm thick.

Use a large gingerbread man form to cut out the Weckmänner. If you don't have a gingerbread man form, roughly sculpt the form of a person with dough. Place raisins where the eyes and buttons should be.

Brush with milk and bake for about 20 minutes or until golden.

Notes

When activating the milk, ensure that the milk is not too warm, but not cold. For me, that meant warming the milk in the microwave for 45 seconds and stirring well to ensure that it was all the same temperature.

Our dough needed approximately 30 minutes to proof. Adjust your time as needed.

Push the raisins into the dough. The dough will rise more with baking, forcing the raisins to pop out (as happened with ours).

Baking time will depend on the size and thickness of the Weckmänner. Don't let them get too dark. If they are darkening and are not yet ready to take out of the oven, cover with aluminium foil and continue baking until ready.

For Saint Nicolaus/Santa you would serve Christmas bread or cookies, for Knecht Ruprecht/Krampus you would serve Weckmann/Krampus bread with a glass of Schnapps.

www.ingramcontent.com/pod-product-compliance
Lightning Source LLC
Chambersburg PA
CBHW061517040426
42450CB00008B/1670